Camden

Swiss Cottage
88 Avenue
London
NW3 3H
020 7974

Libraries

You may return this book to any Camden library.
For a full list please see www.camden.gov.uk

10/19		
4 NOV 2019		

For terms and conditions of library membership
www.camden.gov.uk/libraries

For 24 hour renewals
www.camden.gov.uk/libraries and click renew
(library card and pin number needed)

Tel: 020 7974 4444 for all library enquiries

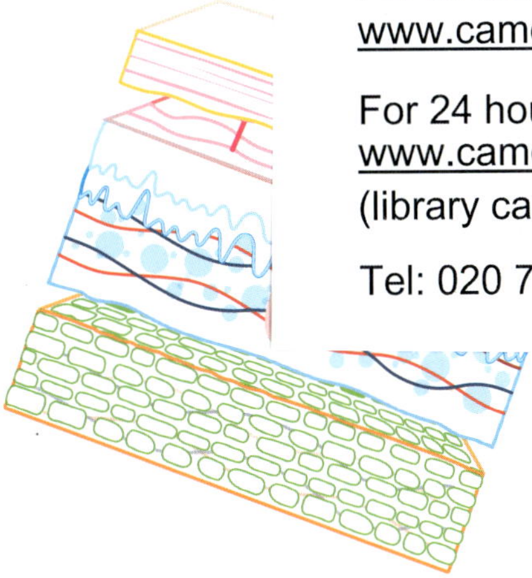

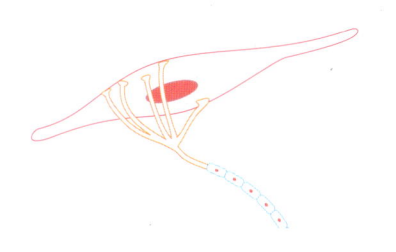

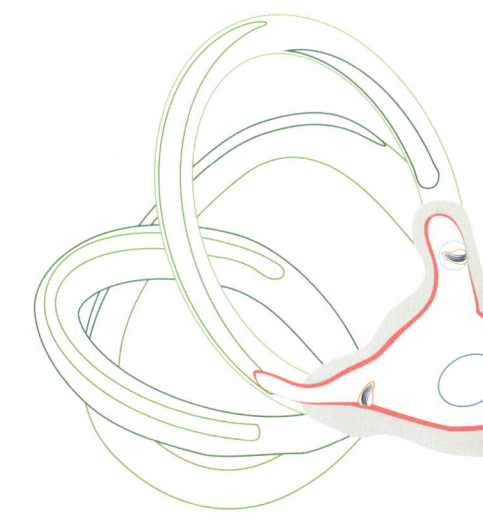

THE SENSES

THE BRIGHT & BOLD HUMAN BODY

IZZI HOWELL

WAYLAND
www.waylandbooks.co.uk

First published in Great Britain in 2019 by Wayland

Copyright © Hodder & Stoughton Limited, 2019

Produced for Wayland by
White-Thomson Publishing Ltd
www.wtpub.co.uk

All rights reserved.

Editor: Izzi Howell
Designer: Dan Prescott, Couper Street Type Co.

HB ISBN: 978 1 5263 1044 6
PB ISBN: 978 1 5263 1043 9
10 9 8 7 6 5 4 3 2 1

Wayland
An imprint of Hachette Children's Group
Part of Hodder & Stoughton
Carmelite House
50 Victoria Embankment
London EC4Y 0DZ

An Hachette UK Company
www.hachette.co.uk
www.hachettechildrens.co.uk

Printed in China

Picture acknowledgements
Getty: normaals 10, STEVE GSCHMEISSNER/SCIENCE PHOTO LIBRARY 11r, BananaStock 17b, ttsz 23t; Shutterstock: metamorworks 4, mimagephotography 5, jehsomwang 6, Johanna Goodyear 7tl, Helenabdullah 7bl, Peter Hermes Furian 7c, Sakurra 7r, pathdoc 9t, Sakurra 11l, Kzenon 13t, trgrowth 13b, VectorMine 14, 21 and 28t, Rocketclips, Inc 15t, gritsalak karalak 16 and 31, Designua 17t, 19t and 25r, solar22 18, puhhha 19b, Dario Lo Presti 20, Nina Puankova 22, Juriah Mosin 23b, ellepigrafica 24, Giovanni Cancemi 25l, Panda Vector 26t, shopplaywood 26l, Pszczola 26r, YanLev 27t, eveleen 27b, ARZTSAMUI 28b; Techtype: 29.

All design elements from Shutterstock.

Every effort has been made to clear copyright. Should there be any inadvertent omission, please apply to the publisher for rectification.

The website addresses (URLs) included in this book were valid at the time of going to press. However, it is possible that contents or addresses may have changed since the publication of this book. No responsibility for any such changes can be accepted by either the author or the publisher.

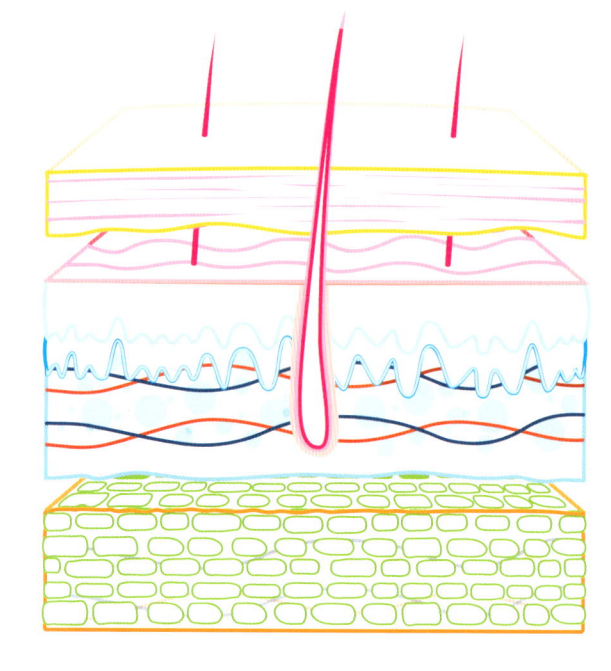

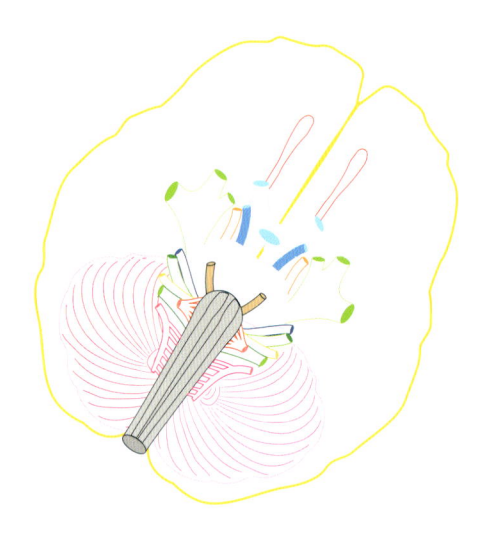

Contents

The senses — 4
Sight — 6
Looking around — 8
Hearing — 10
Different sounds — 12
Taste — 14
Smell — 16
Touch — 18
Sensing pain — 20
Position and balance — 22
Reacting to senses — 24
Internal senses — 26
Problems with senses — 28
Glossary — 30
Further information — 31
Index — 32

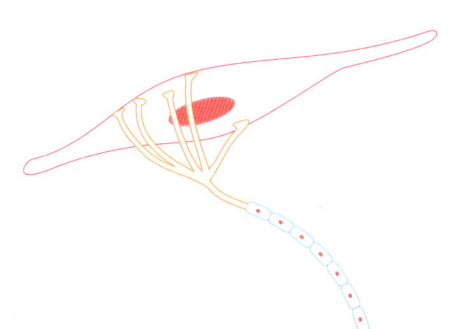

The senses

The five main senses are sight, hearing, taste, smell and touch. They help us to understand our surroundings and keep us safe from danger.

Four of the five organs for sensing are in your head. These include the eyes (sight), the ears (hearing), the nose (smell) and the mouth (taste). Skin all over the body senses touch, but the most sensitive touch receptors are in your fingertips and palms.

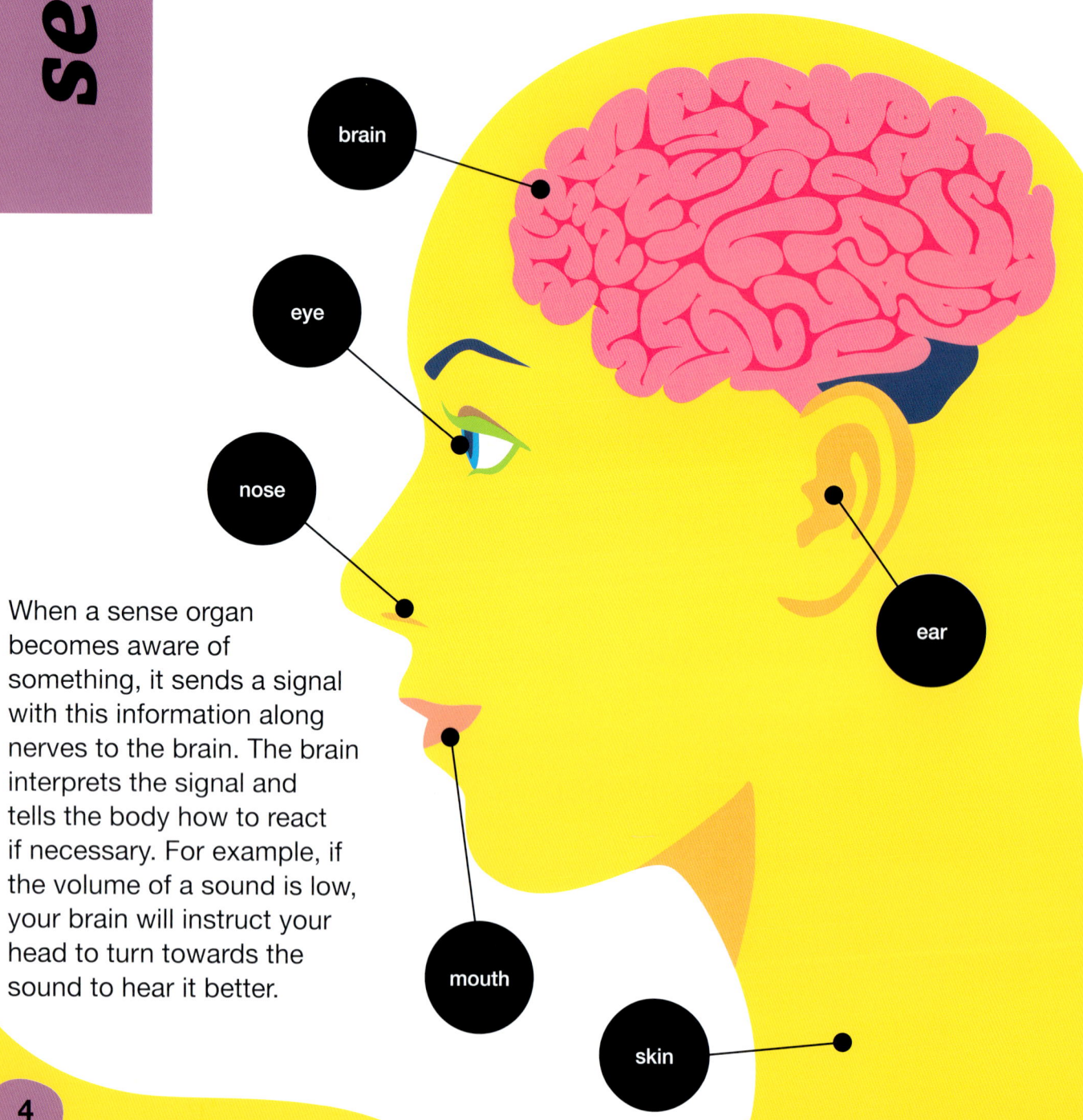

When a sense organ becomes aware of something, it sends a signal with this information along nerves to the brain. The brain interprets the signal and tells the body how to react if necessary. For example, if the volume of a sound is low, your brain will instruct your head to turn towards the sound to hear it better.

- brain
- eye
- nose
- ear
- mouth
- skin

The brain is constantly receiving information from the sense organs, so it blocks out any messages that aren't important. For example, our skin always senses the feeling of the clothes we wear, but the brain doesn't focus on this sensation unless it's important or different, such as an itch or discomfort.

11 million

the number of bits of information that the brain receives from the senses every second

Not everyone senses the same. Blind people, for example, sometimes find that their other senses, such as smell, are stronger than those of sighted people. This is because their brains develop in a different way to make up for their lack of sight.

Sight

Sight is the sense that we use the most to get information about our surroundings. Seeing begins when the eyes detect light. They send this information to the brain, where the light is understood as images.

The eyes are ball-shaped organs that sit in sockets in the head. From the outside, we can see the iris (coloured part), pupil (dark circle in the centre) and sclera (white outer coating), but there is much more to the eye inside the body.

- The retina is the area where light-detecting cells are found.
- The choroid contains arteries and veins to bring blood to and from the eye.
- The optic nerve connects the eye to the brain.
- The sclera protects the inside of the eye.
- The lens is the transparent internal part of the eye.
- The iris can be blue, green, brown or a combination of these colours.
- The pupil is actually a hole in the centre of the iris, although it looks like a dark circle.
- The cornea is the transparent front layer of the eye.
- The vitreous body is a clear gel that fills the inside of the eye. It helps the eye to keep its shape.

80% the percentage of the information we receive that comes through sight

6

Rods (in blue) are sensitive to black and white light and to dim light. They are used for night vision.

Cones (in pink) are sensitive to bright and coloured light.

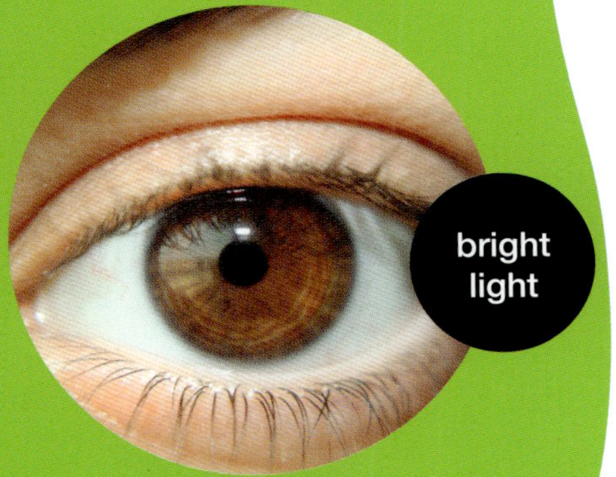

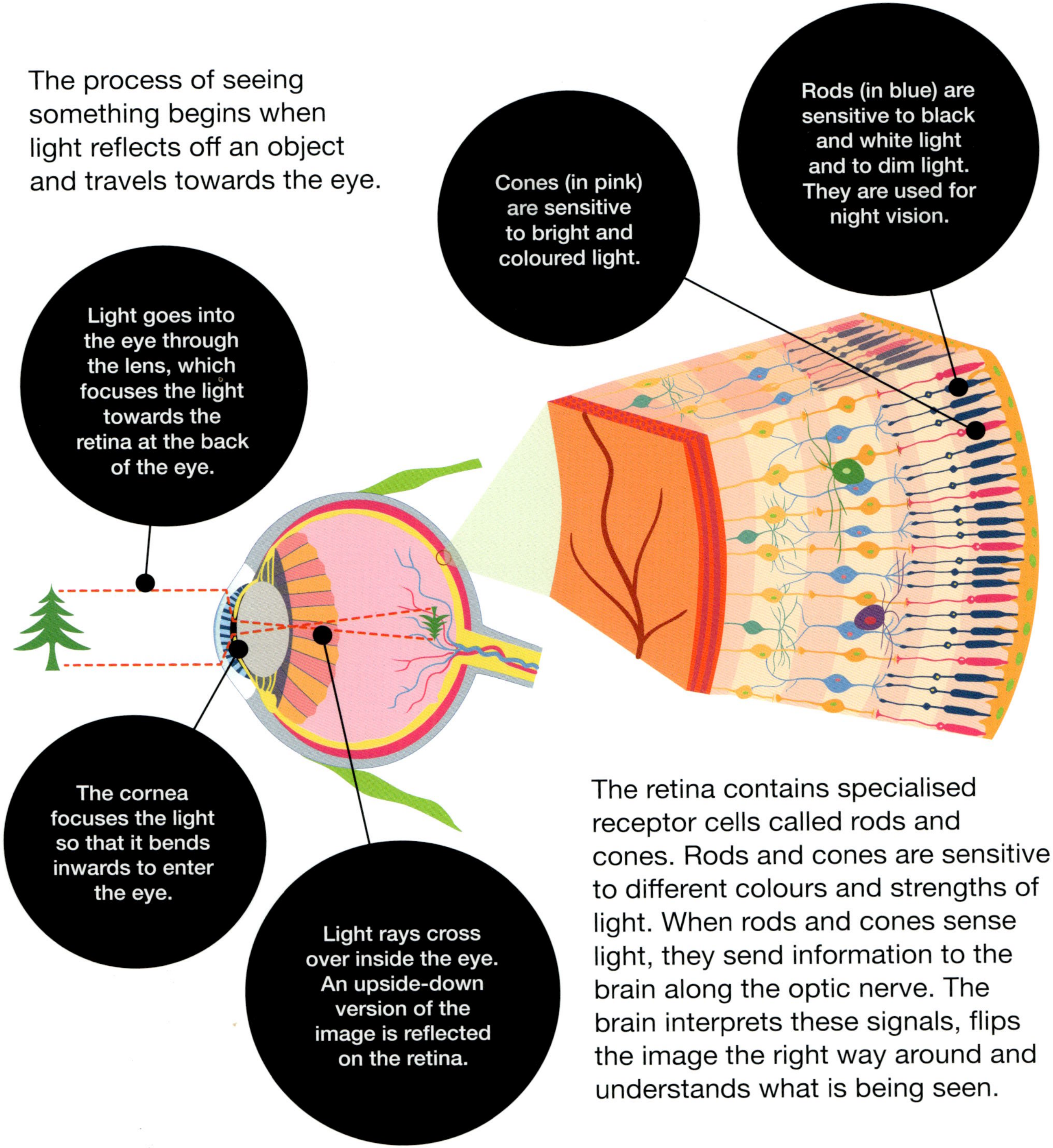

The retina contains specialised receptor cells called rods and cones. Rods and cones are sensitive to different colours and strengths of light. When rods and cones sense light, they send information to the brain along the optic nerve. The brain interprets these signals, flips the image the right way around and understands what is being seen.

The process of seeing something begins when light reflects off an object and travels towards the eye.

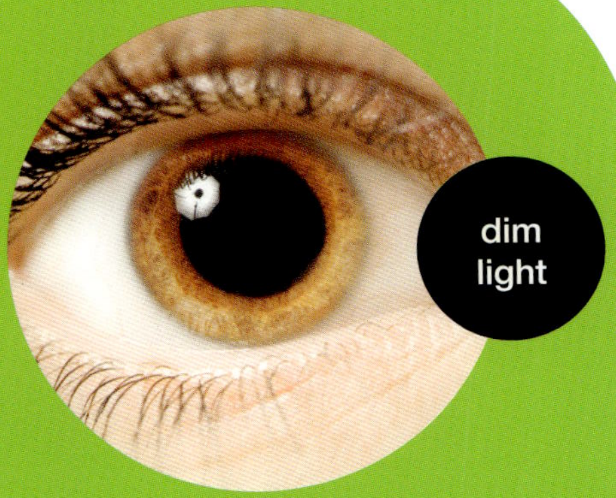

Light rays cross over inside the eye. An upside-down version of the image is reflected on the retina.

Light goes into the eye through the lens, which focuses the light towards the retina at the back of the eye.

The cornea focuses the light so that it bends inwards to enter the eye.

dim light

bright light

The pupil gets bigger or smaller depending on the amount of light. In dim light, the pupil gets bigger to let more light into the eye. In bright light, it gets smaller as less light is needed and too much light can be damaging.

7

Looking around

The structure and position of the eyes allow us to see beyond what is directly in front of us. They also give us a sense of depth to understand the position of objects.

Muscles around the eyes allow us to move them to different positions. This increases our field of vision (the area that we can see). We wouldn't normally be aware of objects above, below or to either side of our head, but we can see these areas if we move our eyes to different positions. There are limits, however, as we need to move our head to see objects behind us.

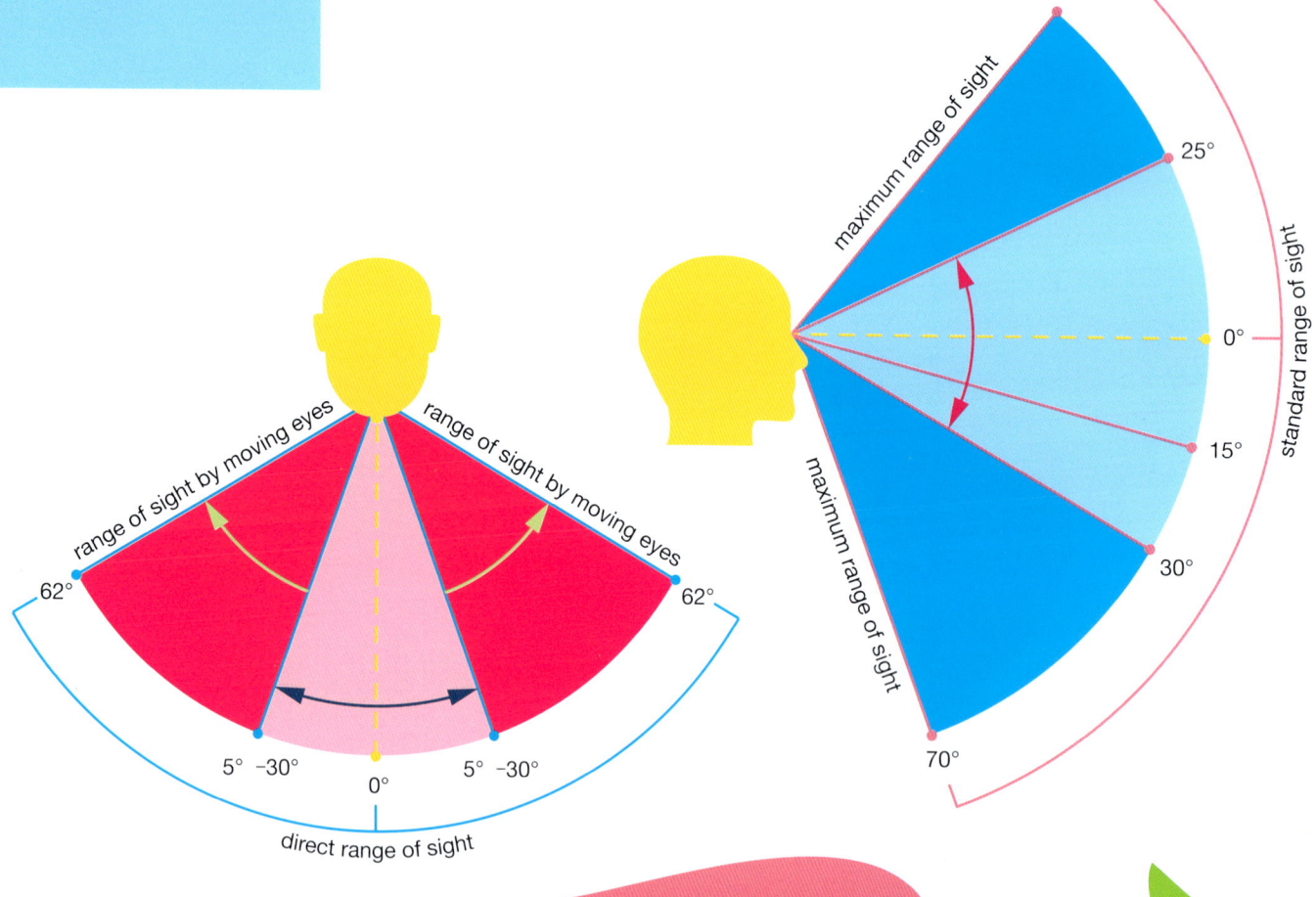

range of sight by moving eyes
62° 62°
5° −30° 0° 5° −30°
direct range of sight

maximum range of sight
50°
25°
0°
15°
30°
70°
standard range of sight
maximum range of sight

nearly 360°

the field of vision of a rabbit, which helps them spot predators in all directions

8

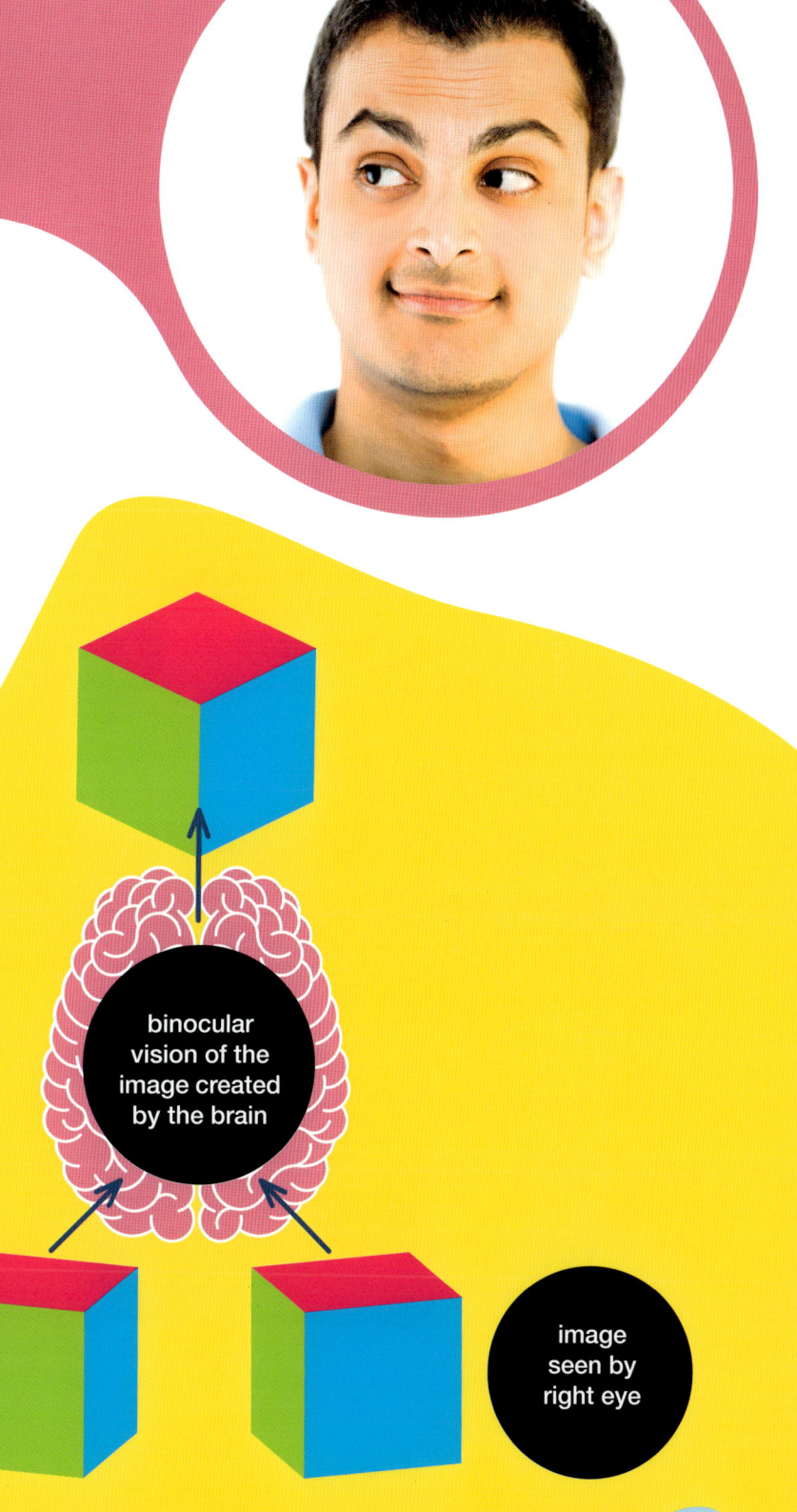

Both eyes move when we look at an object to the side, but only the eye closest to that side can actually see the object.

Because our eyes are in different positions, each eye receives a slightly different image of objects in front of it. The brain combines these two versions into one single 3D image, in which we have a sense of depth. This is called binocular vision. It helps us to understand how close objects are to us, which is very important for actions, such as walking through a crowd, driving, throwing and catching.

binocular vision of the image created by the brain

image seen by left eye

image seen by right eye

Hearing

Sound travels in waves of vibration. Organs inside the ear change these waves into signals that are sent on to the brain. The brain understands them as sounds or speech.

Sound waves travel down the ear canal to the middle ear. This area contains a thin membrane called an ear drum and three tiny bones called the incus, malleus and stapes. When sound waves hit the ear drum, it vibrates. The vibrations pass on to the tiny bones, which move as a result.

- semicircular canals
- incus, malleus and stapes bones
- vestibular nerve
- auditory nerve
- outer ear
- ear canal
- ear drum
- cochlea

The outer ear is outside the body. It has a gently funnelled shape that guides sound waves into the ear.

0.05 seconds

the amount of time it takes for someone to recognise a sound once it enters the ear, making it the fastest human sense

Vibrations from the middle ear travel on to the inner ear. The inner ear is deep inside the body. It contains the cochlea, semicircular canals (see page 23) and nerves that go to the brain. The cochlea is a spiral-shaped organ, filled with fluid. Inside the cochlea is a section called the organ of Corti, which has sensitive hair receptor cells on its walls. When the hair receptor cells sense vibrations, they convert this information into an electrical signal. The signal travels from the cochlea to the brain along the cochlear nerve.

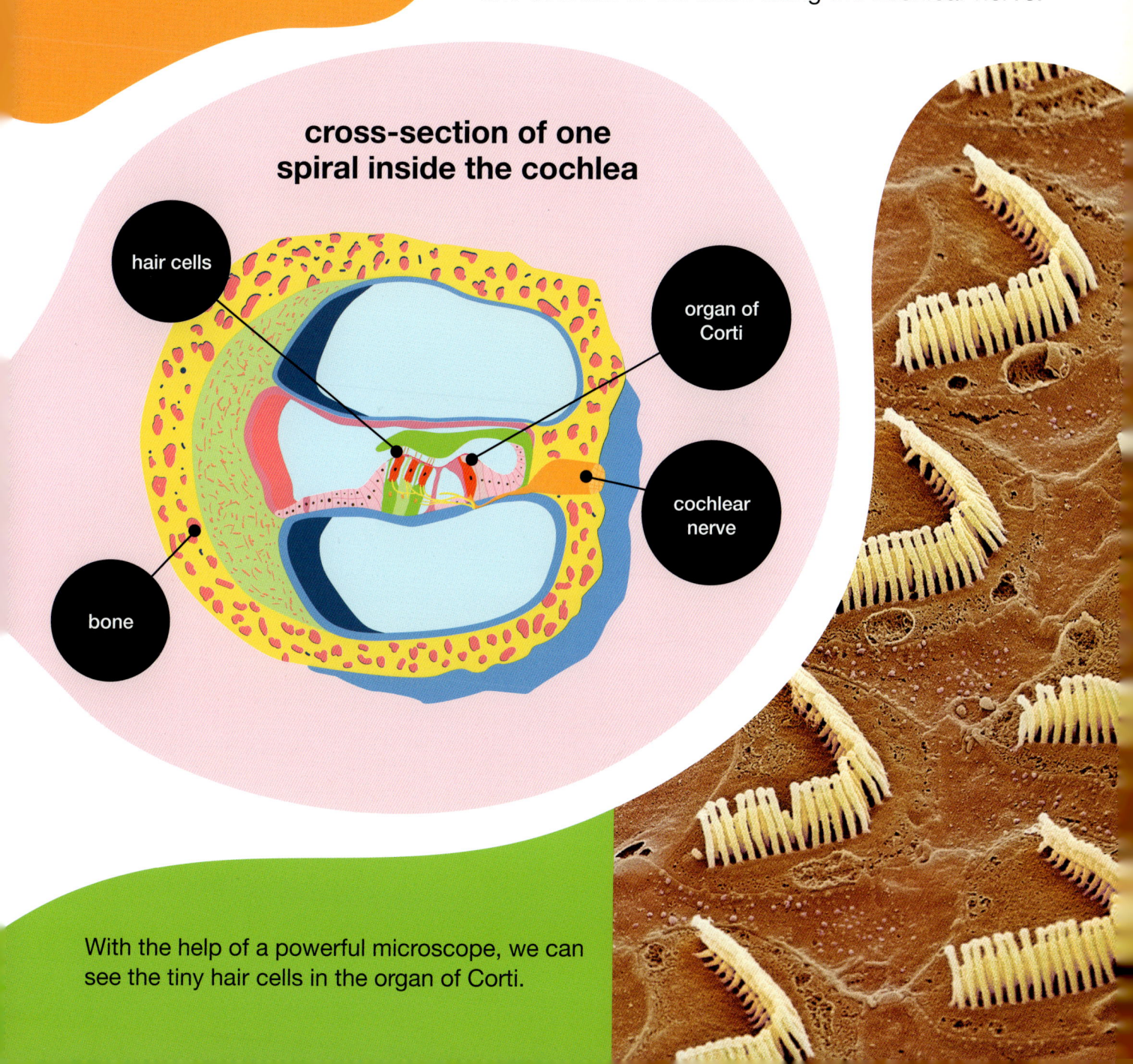

cross-section of one spiral inside the cochlea

- hair cells
- organ of Corti
- cochlear nerve
- bone

With the help of a powerful microscope, we can see the tiny hair cells in the organ of Corti.

Different sounds

There are many types of sound – loud and quiet, high and low. However, the range of human hearing is limited, and we can't hear every sound.

Sound waves are different for high- and low-pitched sounds, as well as for loud and quiet sounds. We can see these differences if we track the vibrations on a machine.

The louder a sound, the more energy it has. Loud sounds make tall waves with a high amplitude (distance from the rest position to the top of the wave). Quiet sounds have less energy, so they result in short waves with low amplitude.

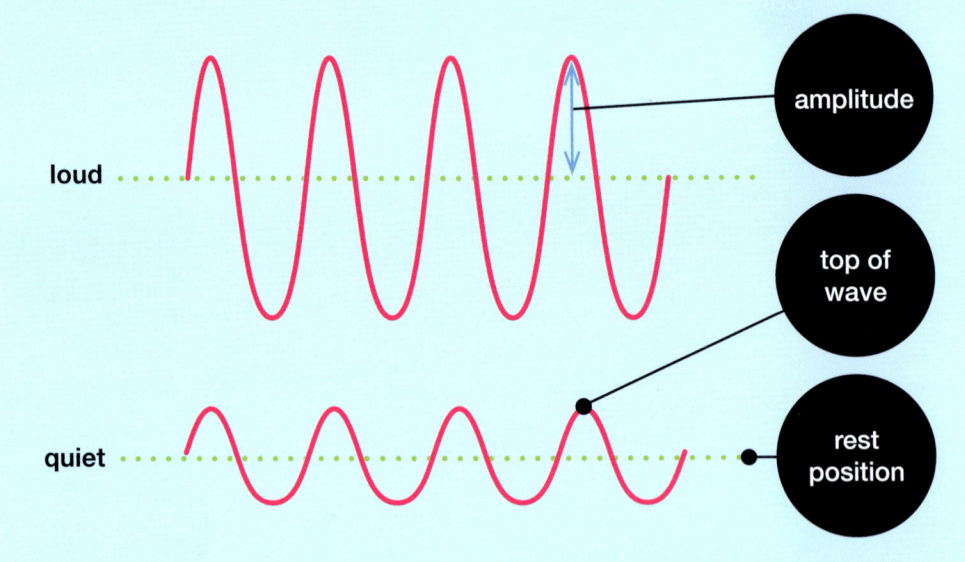

loud

quiet

- amplitude
- top of wave
- rest position

Pitch is how high or low a sound is. It affects the speed of vibration. High-pitched sounds come from quick vibrations, in which the waves are close together. Low-pitched sounds come from slow vibrations, in which the waves are far apart.

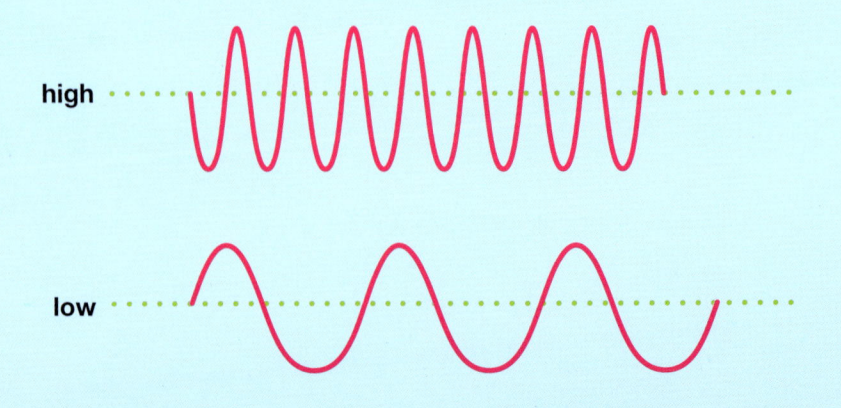

high

low

There are some high and low pitches that humans can't hear because the cochlea isn't sensitive enough. There are also sounds that are too quiet for us to hear. We must avoid very loud sounds, as they can damage our hearing.

Loudness is measured in decibels (dB). People with hearing loss (see page 29) may not be able to hear sounds at the lower end of the scale.

It is important to wear ear defenders to protect your ears from loud noises if you are working with noisy machines.

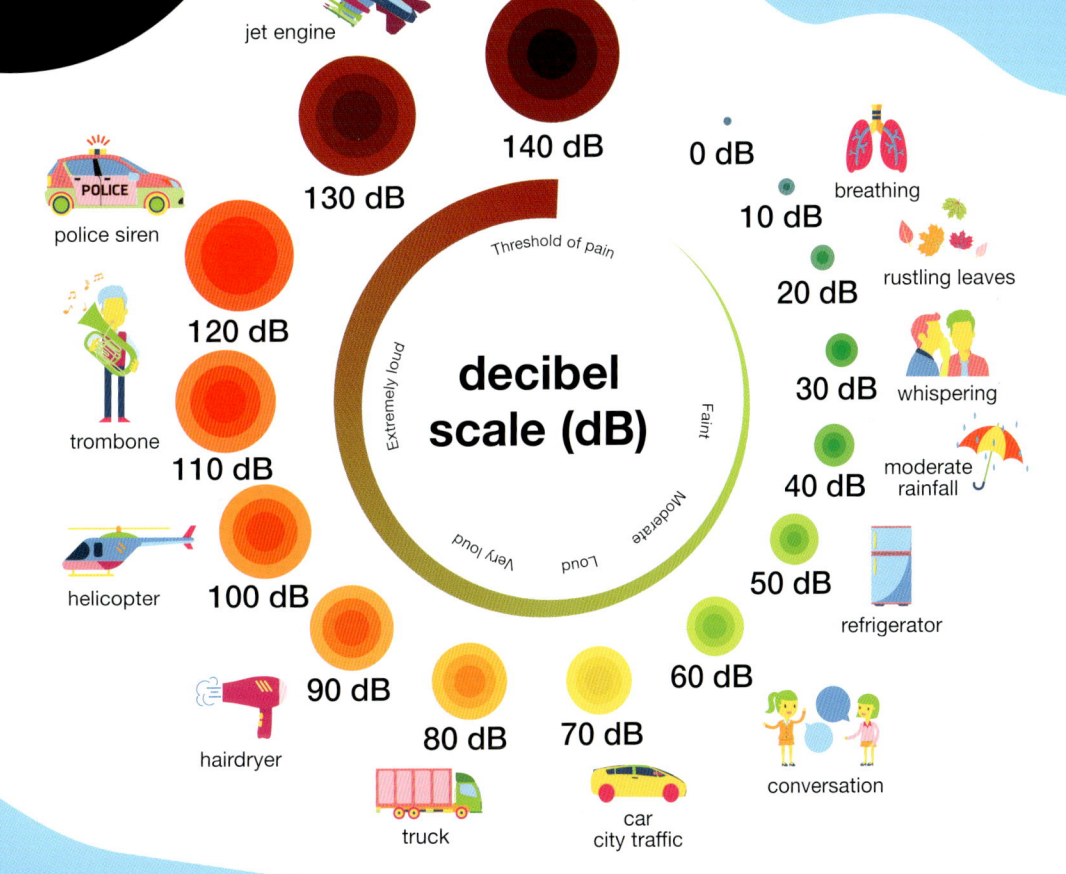

decibel scale (dB)

- 140 dB — fireworks
- 130 dB — jet engine
- 120 dB — police siren
- 110 dB — trombone
- 100 dB — helicopter
- 90 dB — hairdryer
- 80 dB — truck
- 70 dB — car, city traffic
- 60 dB — conversation
- 50 dB — refrigerator
- 40 dB — moderate rainfall
- 30 dB — whispering
- 20 dB — rustling leaves
- 10 dB
- 0 dB — breathing

Threshold of pain · Extremely loud · Very loud · Loud · Moderate · Faint

20,000 hertz (Hz)
the highest pitched sounds that humans can hear, compared to the maximum 150,000 Hz that dolphins can hear

Taste

The sense of taste happens in the mouth. As well as bringing us pleasure through eating, the sense of taste also helps to protect the body. It warns us against poisonous or rotten foods that may make us ill.

The tongue is covered with thousands of tiny bumps called papillae (singular papilla). On each papilla are hundreds of taste buds. Taste buds contain taste receptor cells that recognise different chemicals in food. The inner cheeks, inside of the lips, back and roof of the mouth are also covered in taste buds.

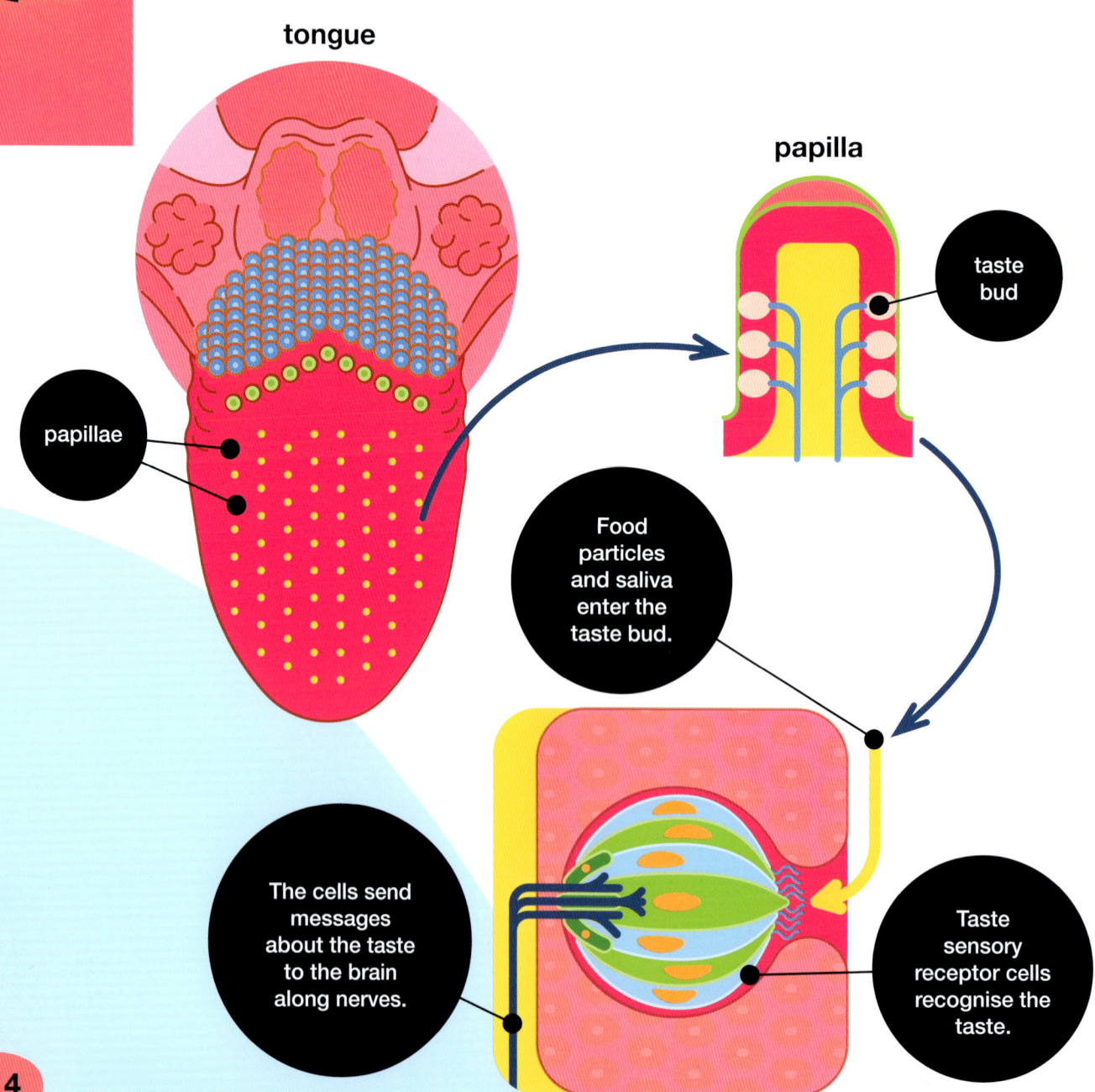

tongue

papilla

papillae

taste bud

Food particles and saliva enter the taste bud.

Taste sensory receptor cells recognise the taste.

The cells send messages about the taste to the brain along nerves.

14

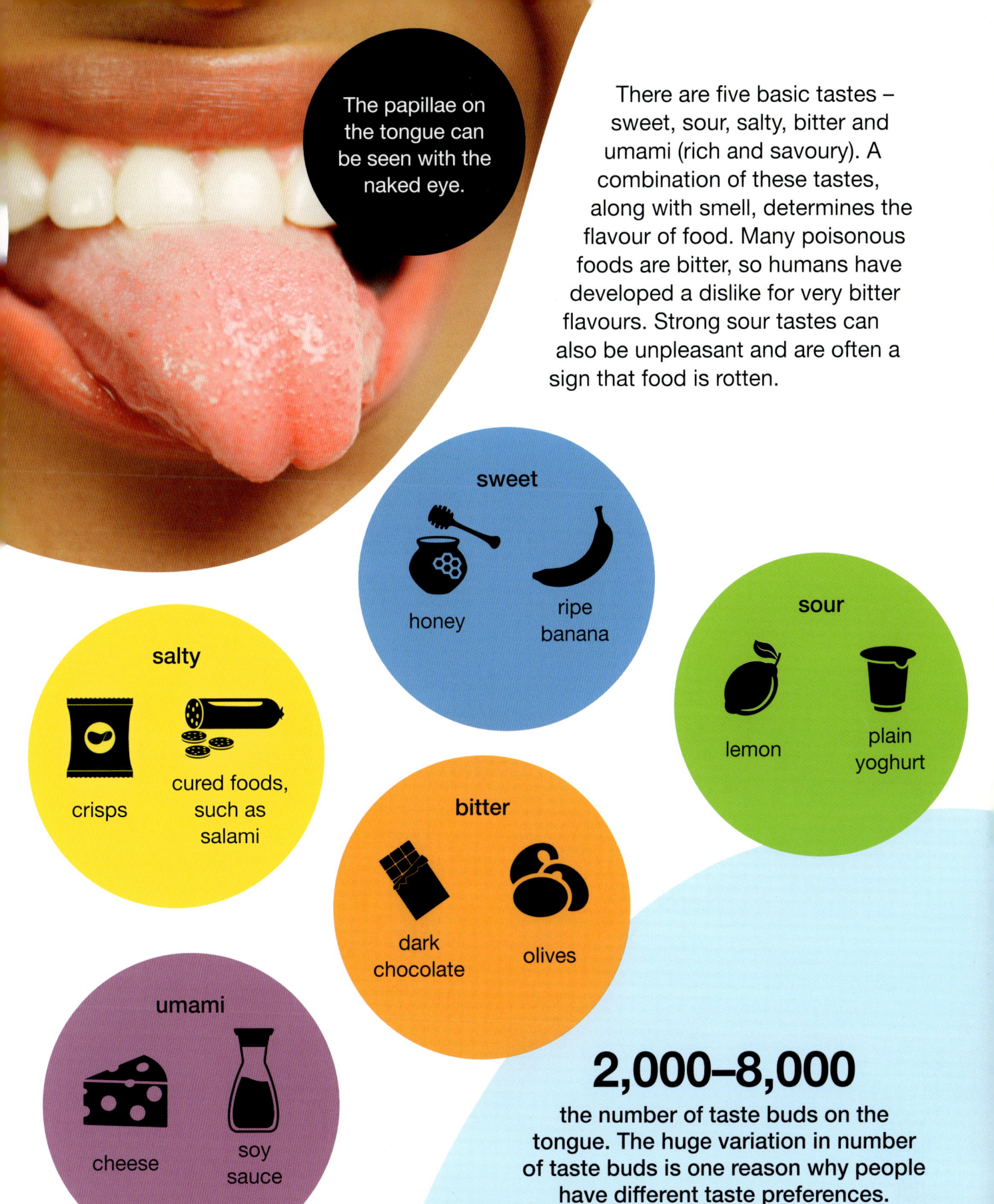

The papillae on the tongue can be seen with the naked eye.

There are five basic tastes – sweet, sour, salty, bitter and umami (rich and savoury). A combination of these tastes, along with smell, determines the flavour of food. Many poisonous foods are bitter, so humans have developed a dislike for very bitter flavours. Strong sour tastes can also be unpleasant and are often a sign that food is rotten.

sweet
honey
ripe banana

sour
lemon
plain yoghurt

salty
crisps
cured foods, such as salami

bitter
dark chocolate
olives

umami
cheese
soy sauce

2,000–8,000

the number of taste buds on the tongue. The huge variation in number of taste buds is one reason why people have different taste preferences.

Smell

Our sense of smell allows us to identify millions of different smells. Some are pleasant, while others, such as poisonous gases and rotten stenches, are warnings.

Some objects release odour molecules that transmit their smell. These molecules are very small and light, so they float easily through the air. We breathe them in accidentally or on purpose when we sniff through our nose. The odour molecules travel through the nostrils into the nose.

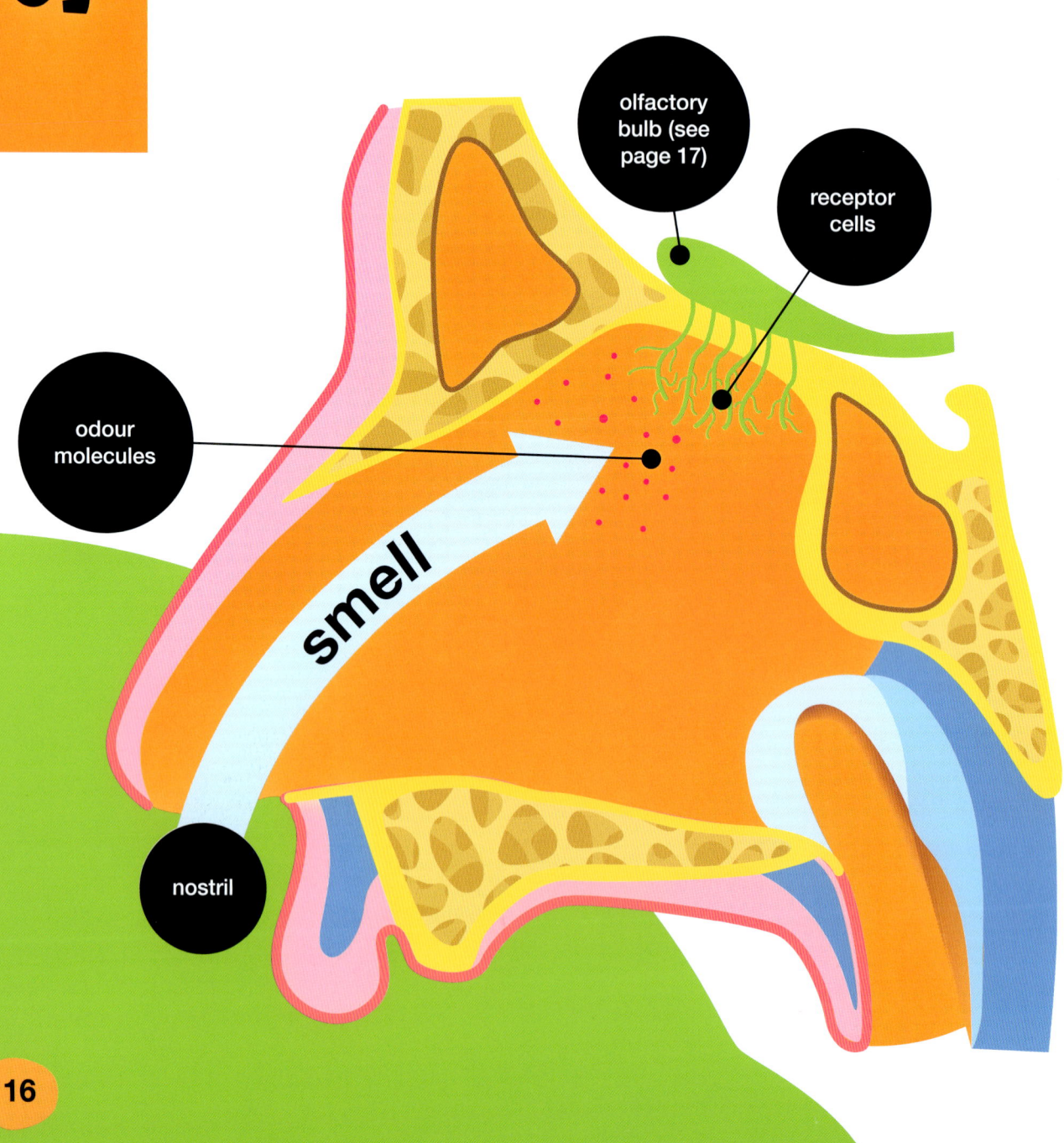

- olfactory bulb (see page 17)
- receptor cells
- odour molecules
- smell
- nostril

Smell receptor cells are found inside the nose at the top of each nostril. The cells have special hair-like endings called cilia, which recognise odour molecules and send a message to an area known as the olfactory bulb. The olfactory bulb passes these messages on to the brain, where they are understood as smells.

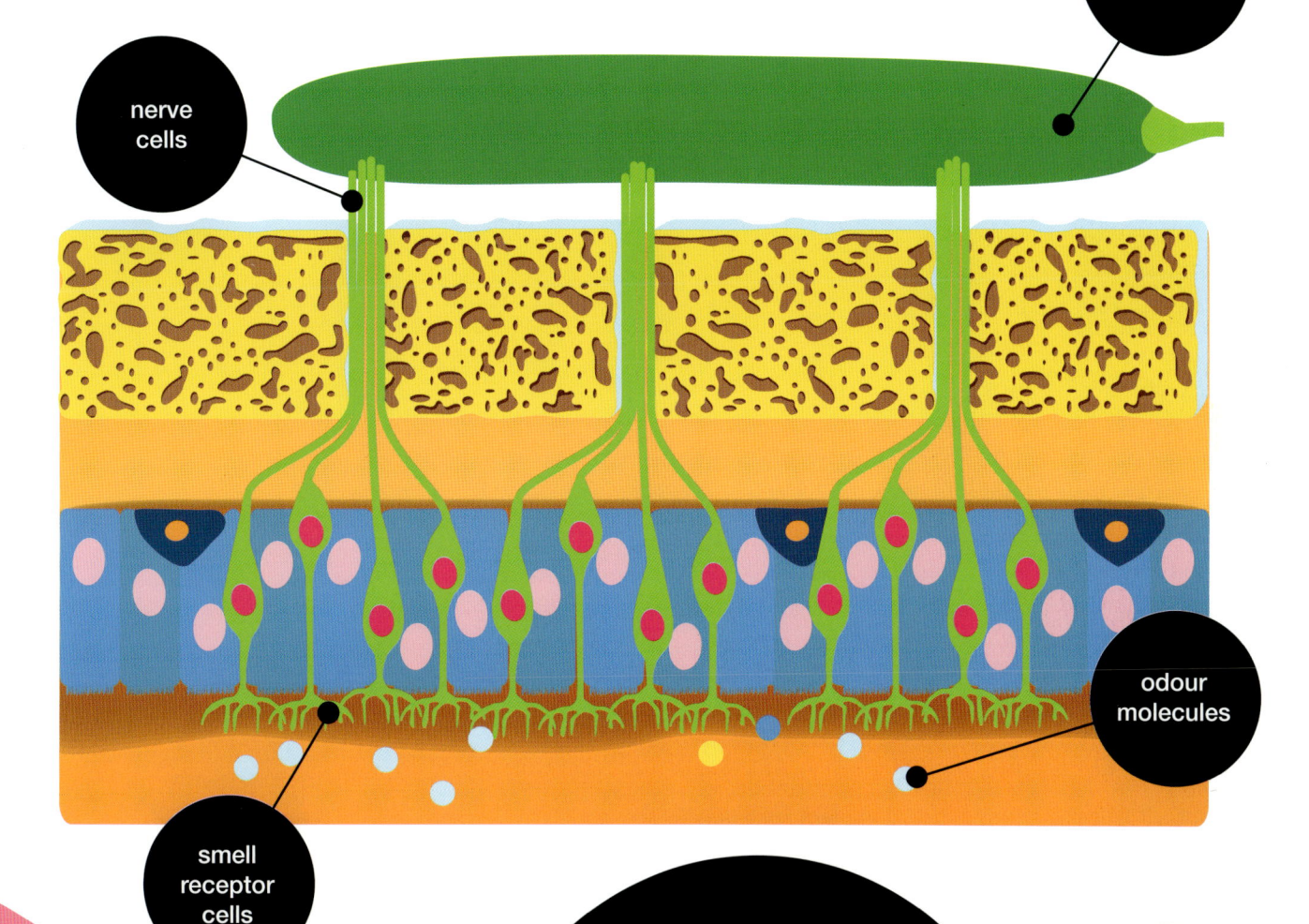

olfactory bulb

nerve cells

odour molecules

smell receptor cells

10,000
the number of times more sensitive the sense of smell is than the sense of taste

When you have a cold, you lose some of your sense of smell because your nose is blocked and odour molecules cannot reach the receptor cells. Smell also contributes to your sense of taste, which is why taste is affected when you have a cold.

Touch

Our skin gives us lots of information about the world around us. It contains special touch receptor cells that recognise texture, pressure, temperature and pain.

The skin is made up of three main layers. The outer layer is called the epidermis, the middle layer is called the dermis and the bottom layer is called the hypodermis.

The epidermis is a barrier that stops bacteria and viruses from entering the body. It also contains tiny holes called pores through which sweat leaves the body.

Blood vessels and most touch receptor cells are found in the dermis. It also contains the roots of the hairs that cover our skin, and sweat glands that produce sweat.

The hypodermis contains a layer of fat that helps to keep the body warm. This fat can be burned if we need extra energy.

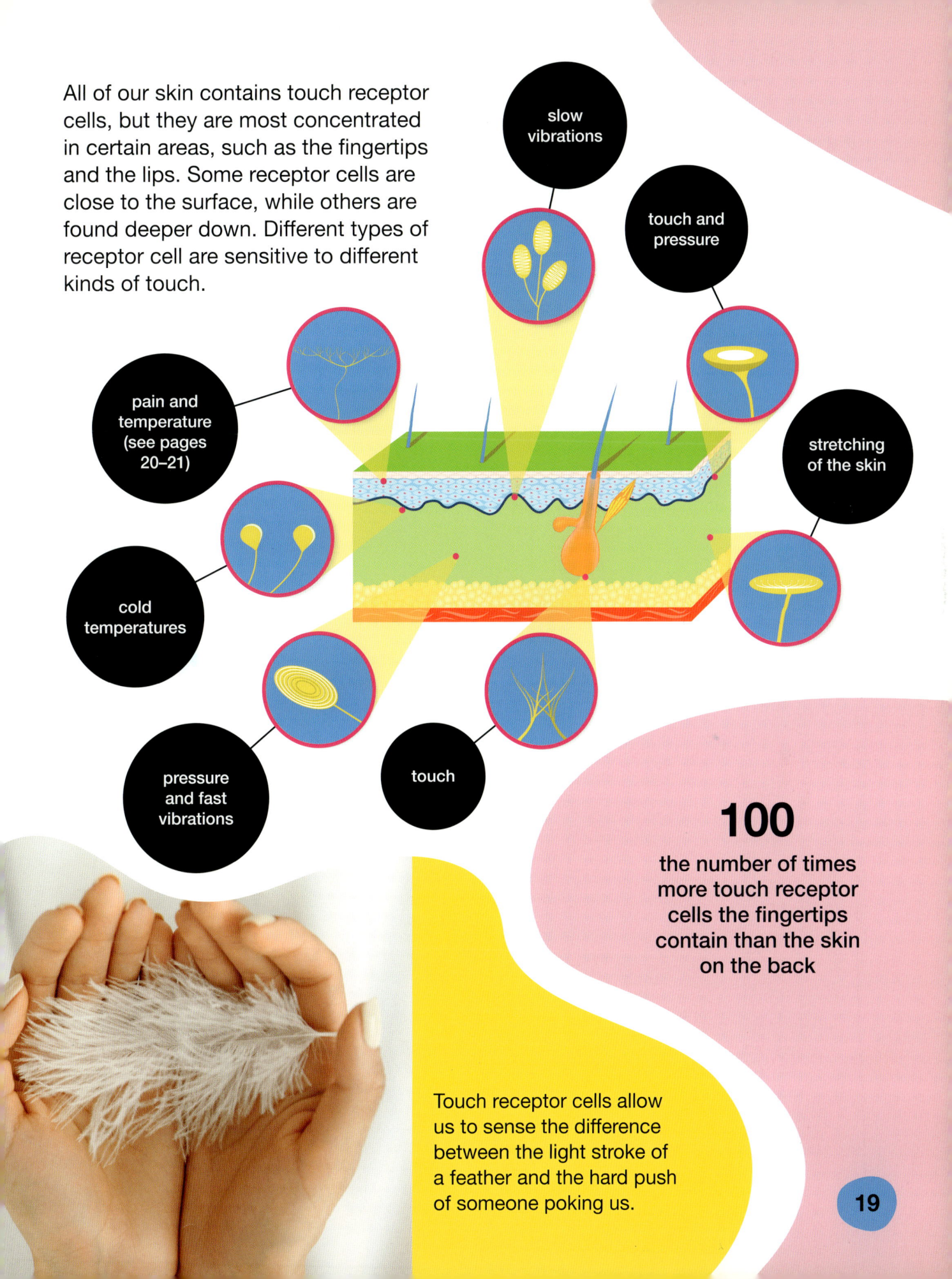

All of our skin contains touch receptor cells, but they are most concentrated in certain areas, such as the fingertips and the lips. Some receptor cells are close to the surface, while others are found deeper down. Different types of receptor cell are sensitive to different kinds of touch.

slow vibrations

touch and pressure

pain and temperature (see pages 20–21)

stretching of the skin

cold temperatures

pressure and fast vibrations

touch

100

the number of times more touch receptor cells the fingertips contain than the skin on the back

Touch receptor cells allow us to sense the difference between the light stroke of a feather and the hard push of someone poking us.

Sensing pain

- low temperatures – freezing sensation
- very spicy foods – burning sensation
- high temperatures – burning sensation
- some poisons – itchy sensation

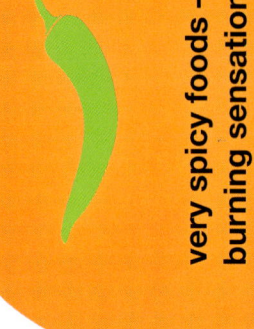

The feeling of pain alerts us to danger. Discomfort lets us know that something is wrong so that we can react and try to stop things from hurting us.

Pain touch receptors aren't only found in the skin – they are also located inside the body in internal organs, muscles and joints. They sense damage done to different parts of the body through injury, illness or infection. We experience this damage as pain, such as a stomach ache or a sore muscle. Other dangers that can harm the body create different sensations.

When you get a cut, the pressure of the object that creates the cut alerts pressure receptor cells. They inform the brain that the skin has been damaged.

200

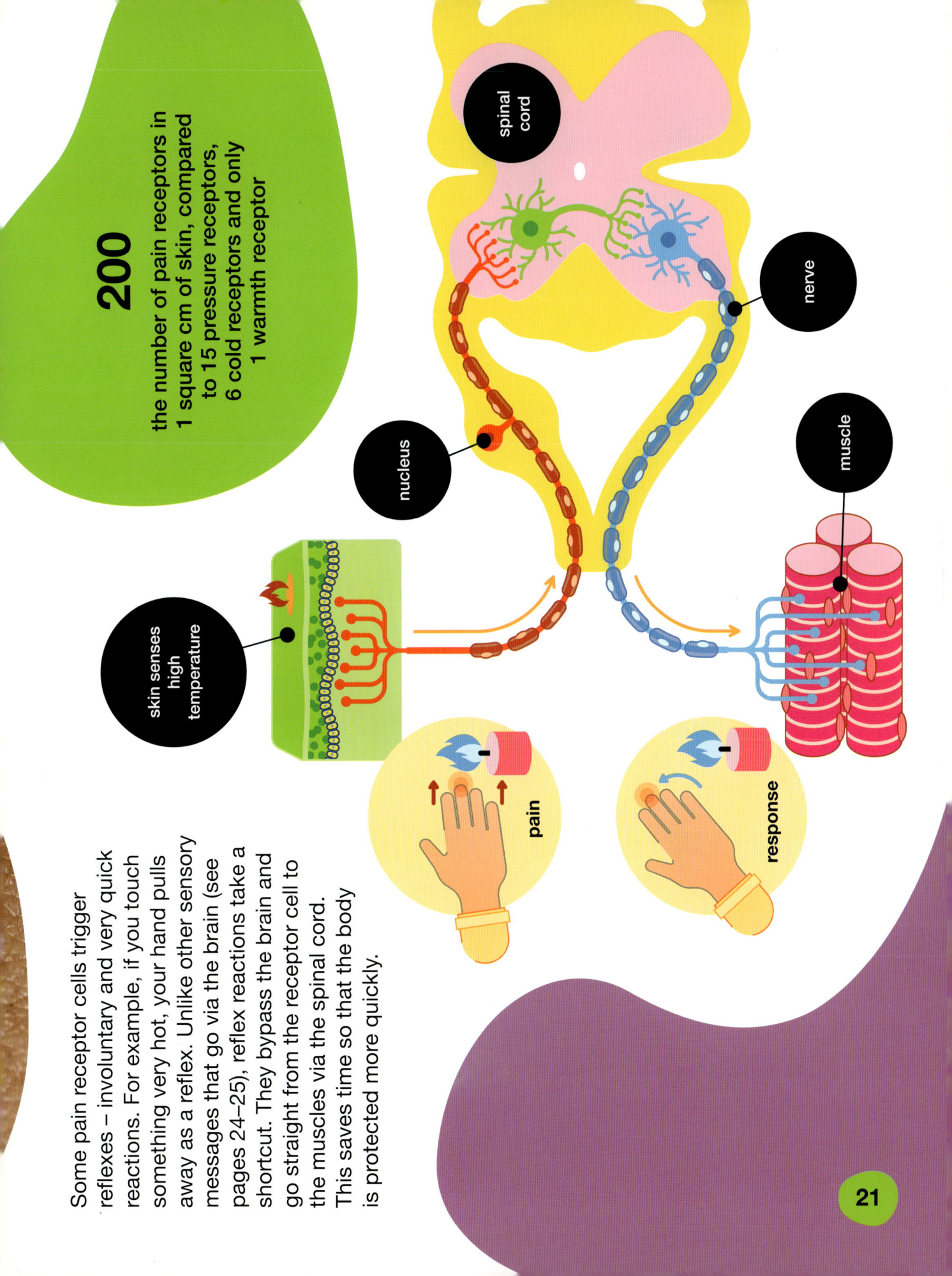

the number of pain receptors in 1 square cm of skin, compared to 15 pressure receptors, 6 cold receptors and only 1 warmth receptor

spinal cord

nerve

nucleus

muscle

skin senses high temperature

pain

response

Some pain receptor cells trigger reflexes – involuntary and very quick reactions. For example, if you touch something very hot, your hand pulls away as a reflex. Unlike other sensory messages that go via the brain (see pages 24–25), reflex reactions take a shortcut. They bypass the brain and go straight from the receptor cell to the muscles via the spinal cord. This saves time so that the body is protected more quickly.

Position and balance

When thinking about the senses, people often forget the awareness of movement, position of the body and the sense of balance. However, these are very important senses.

Proprioception is the sense of knowing where your body is and its position in relation to its environment. Sensory receptor cells in muscles and joints send signals to the brain to give it information about the position of the body without having to look to see where it is. For example, if you close your eyes, you can still touch your nose. This is because your body knows the position of your nose and your arm, and reacts to guide the hand to the nose as it moves through the air. Proprioception allows us to move quickly and easily without having to think about it.

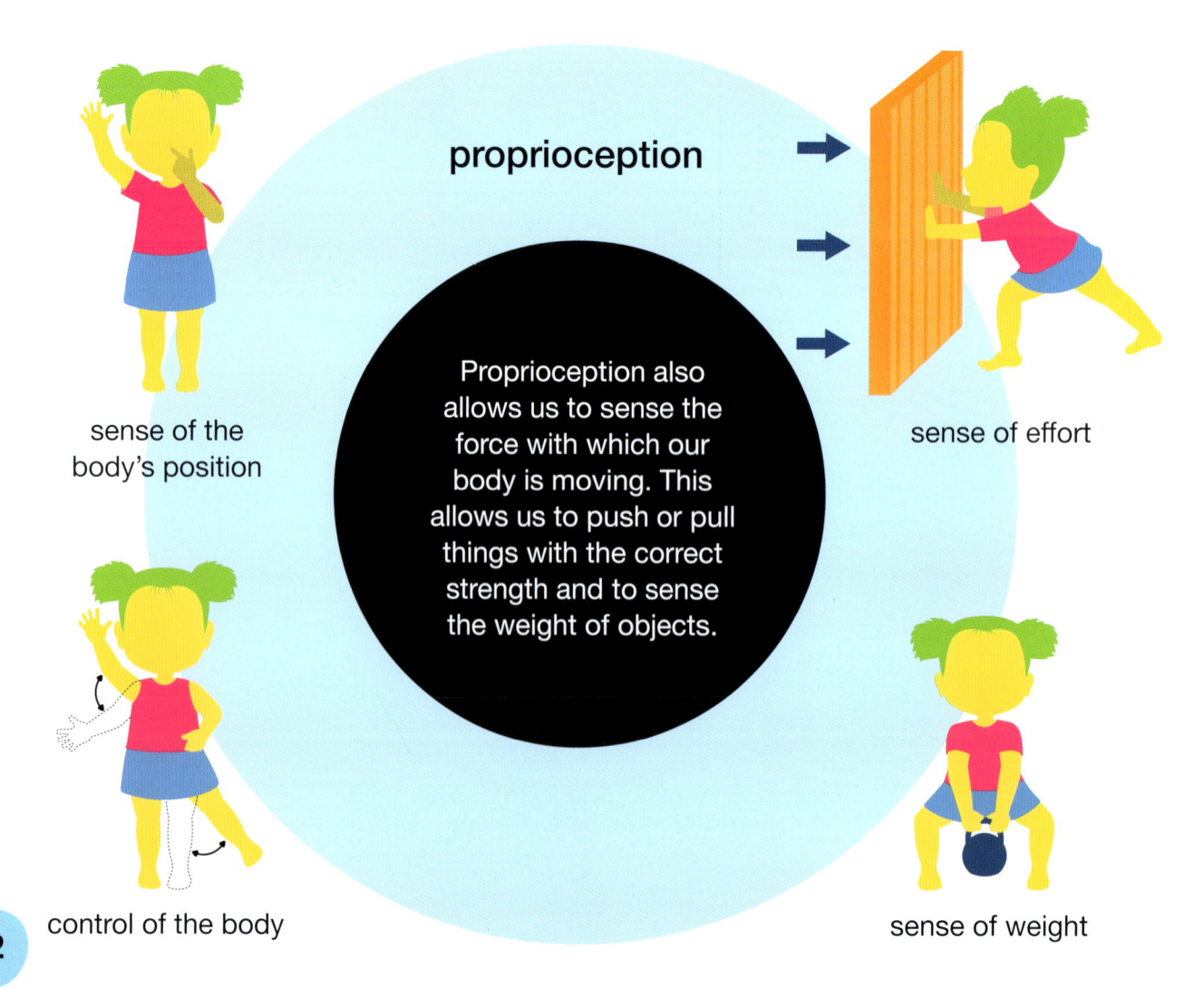

proprioception

Proprioception also allows us to sense the force with which our body is moving. This allows us to push or pull things with the correct strength and to sense the weight of objects.

- sense of the body's position
- sense of effort
- control of the body
- sense of weight

Balance is also related to sense, as sensors in the ears react to changes in position to keep the body upright. These sensors are located in a set of tubes in the inner ear called the semicircular canals. When you move your body, liquid in the tubes moves and bends tiny hairs inside an area called the cupula. The hairs are connected to nerves that send messages to the brain along the vestibular nerve. These messages inform the brain of the position of the body, so that it can instruct the body to move to keep its balance if necessary.

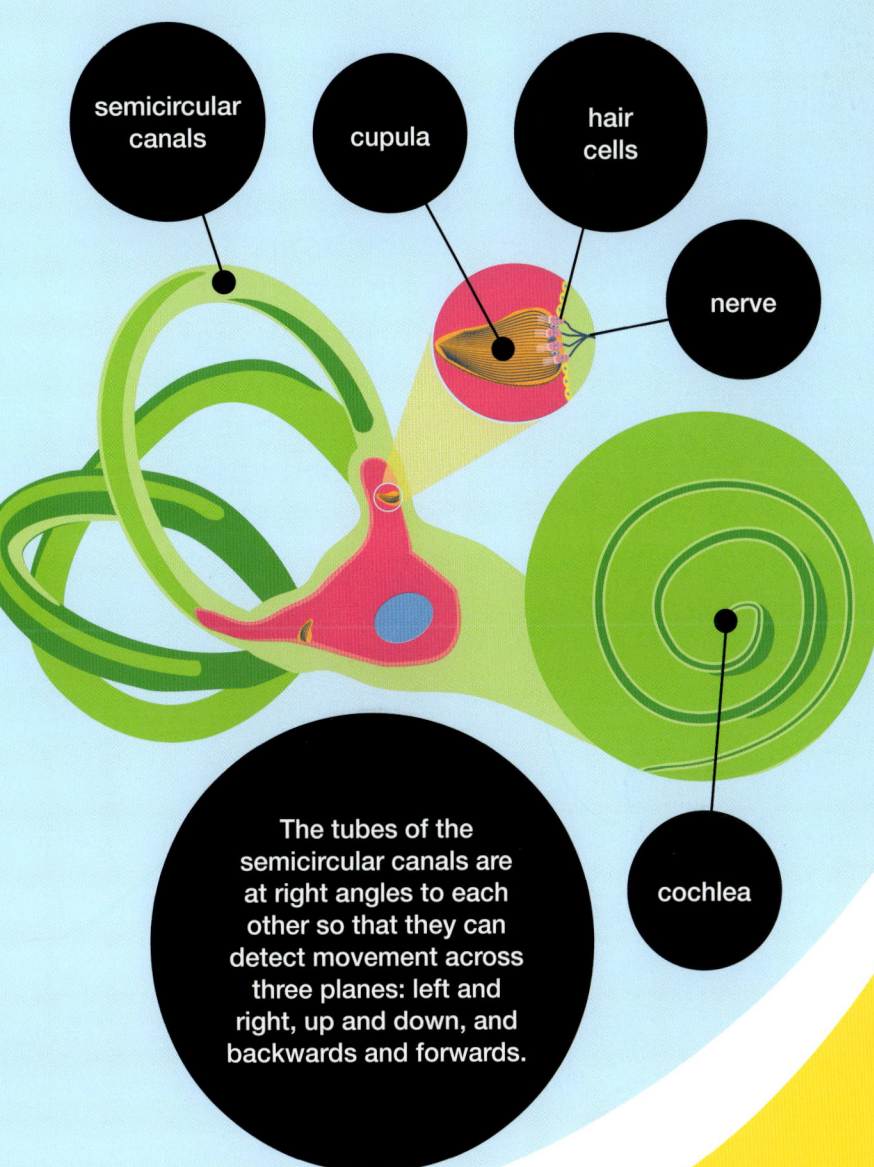

semicircular canals

cupula

hair cells

nerve

cochlea

The tubes of the semicircular canals are at right angles to each other so that they can detect movement across three planes: left and right, up and down, and backwards and forwards.

12–22 mm
the average length of each semicircular canal

Spinning around makes you feel dizzy because the movement makes the liquid in the semicircular tubes slosh around. This sends many signals to the brain, which take a while to be interpreted. This produces a dizzy feeling.

Reacting to senses

Information from receptor cells in the sensory organs travels along nerves to the brain. The brain interprets the information and reacts, if necessary, by sending out messages to parts of the body through the nervous system.

The four sensory organs on the face (the ears, eyes, nose and mouth) send information straight into the brainstem (a part of the brain) along cranial nerves in the head. Other sensory cells, such as those in the skin, send information along long nerves in the body. The information goes into the spinal cord and then travels up into the brain.

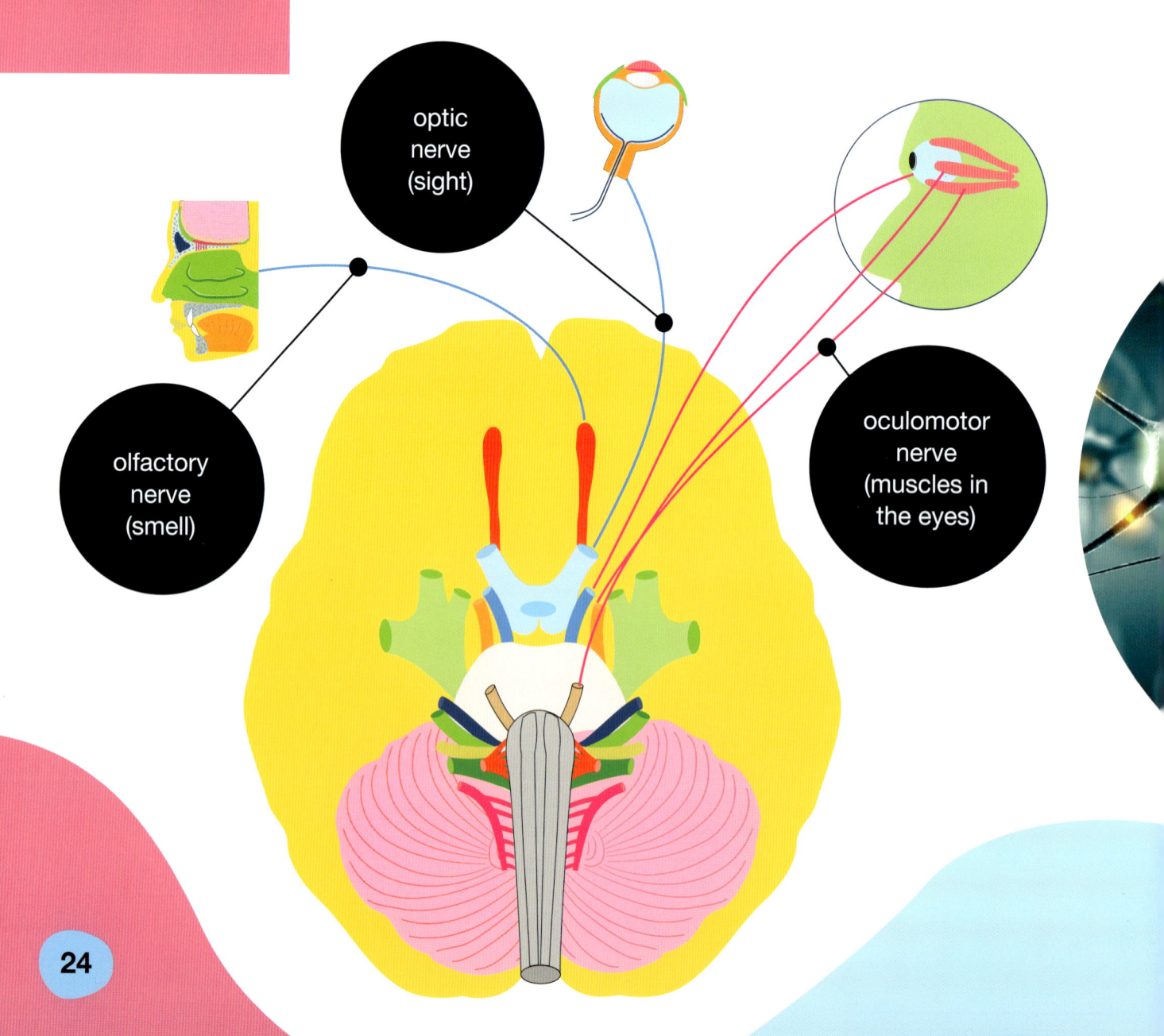

optic nerve (sight)

olfactory nerve (smell)

oculomotor nerve (muscles in the eyes)

24

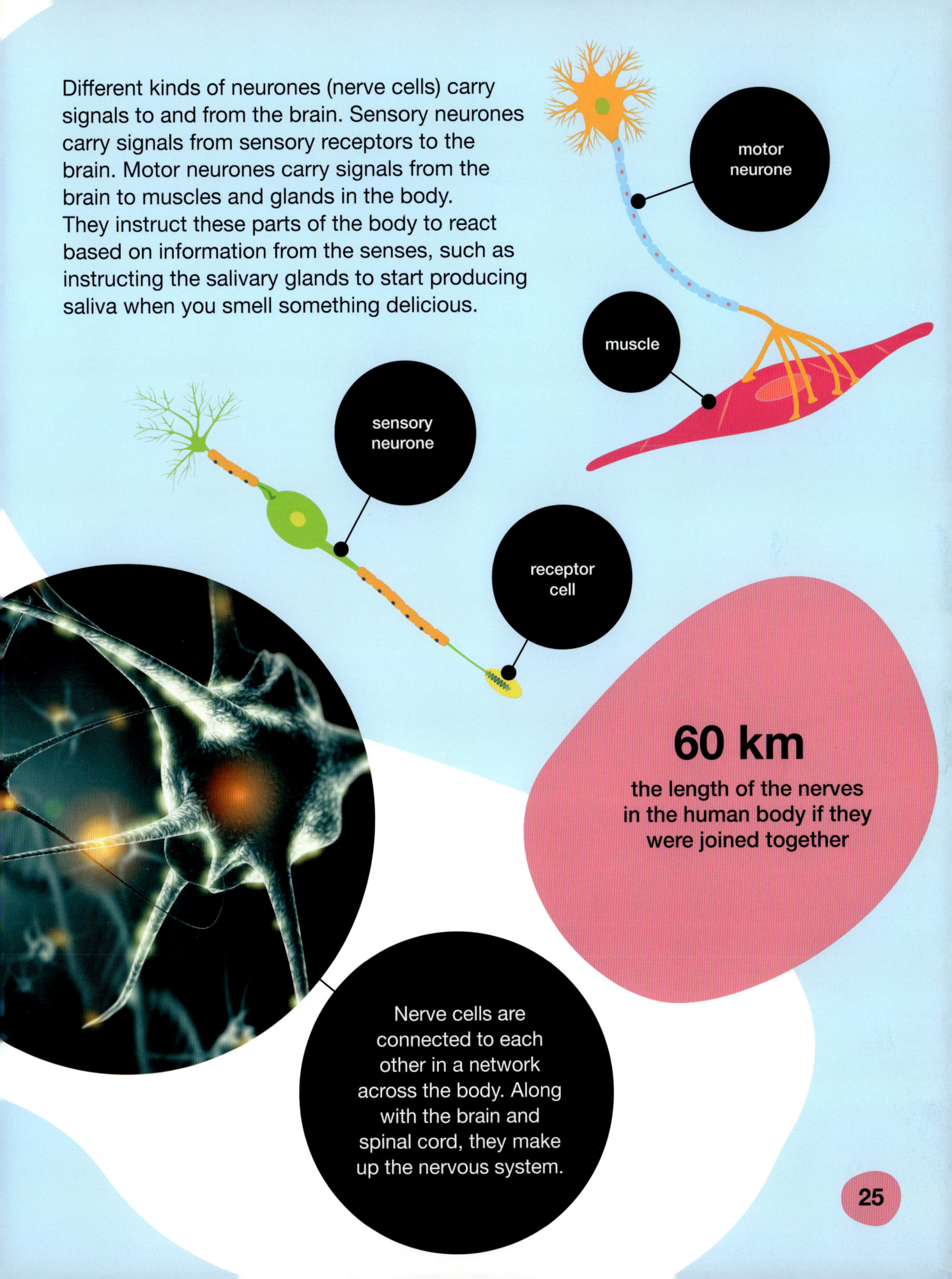

Different kinds of neurones (nerve cells) carry signals to and from the brain. Sensory neurones carry signals from sensory receptors to the brain. Motor neurones carry signals from the brain to muscles and glands in the body. They instruct these parts of the body to react based on information from the senses, such as instructing the salivary glands to start producing saliva when you smell something delicious.

motor neurone

muscle

sensory neurone

receptor cell

60 km
the length of the nerves in the human body if they were joined together

Nerve cells are connected to each other in a network across the body. Along with the brain and spinal cord, they make up the nervous system.

Internal senses

As well as the five main senses that let us know what is going on outside our body, we also rely on internal senses to give us information about what is going on inside the body.

Chemical receptors in different parts of the body monitor the levels of chemicals in the blood. For example, if you stop breathing, or aren't breathing enough, chemical receptors in the blood vessels detect that there isn't enough oxygen in the blood (or that there is too much carbon dioxide). You experience feelings of dizziness and suffocation and you know it is important to start breathing again.

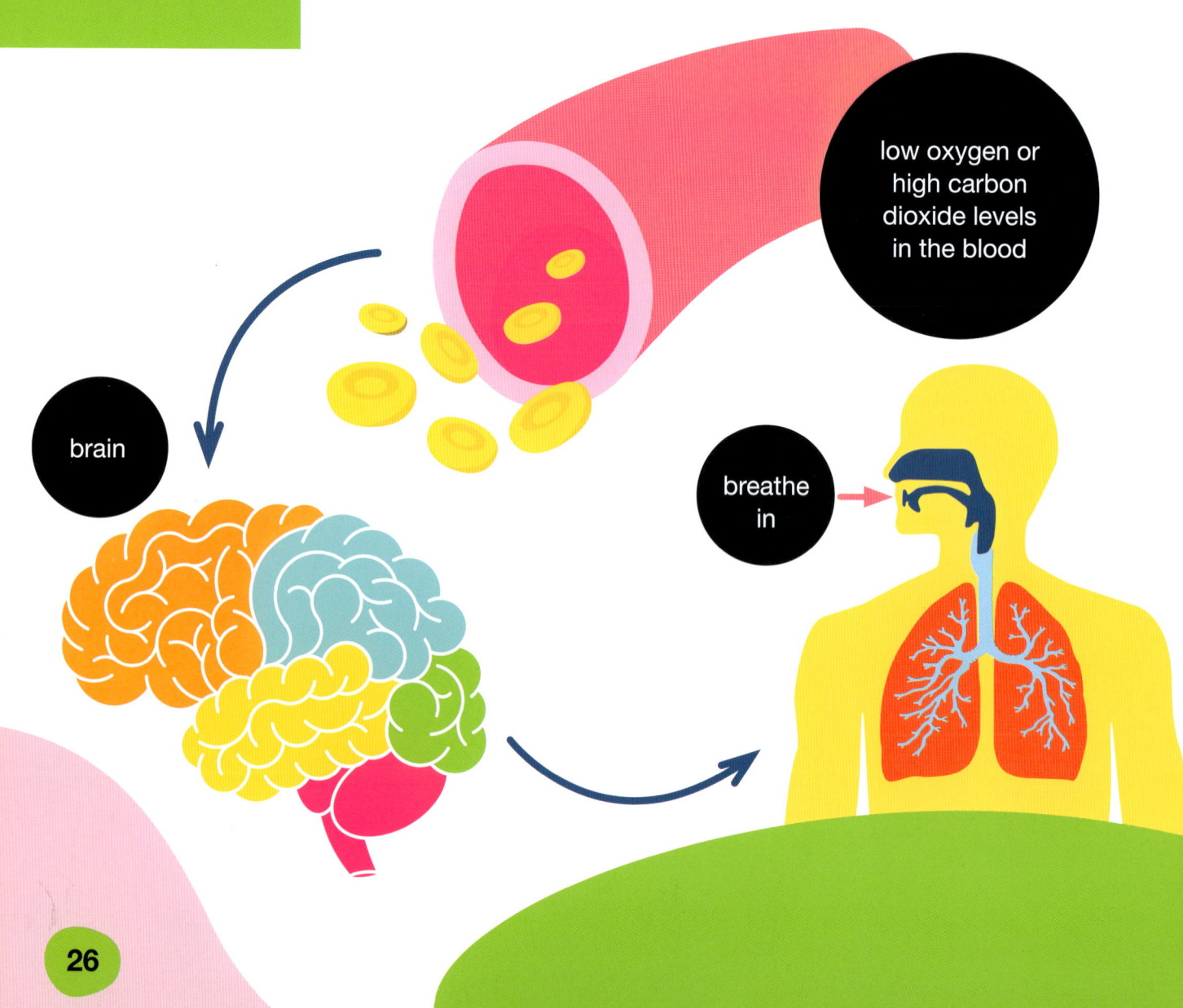

low oxygen or high carbon dioxide levels in the blood

brain

breathe in

You may have experienced feelings of dizziness when your breath runs out underwater. This lets you know that you need to come back to the surface to breathe.

Some internal organs send messages to the brain to report when they are full.

As food fills the stomach, sensors in the walls of the stomach feel it stretching and send messages to the brain. The brain helps to create a feeling of fullness so that we know to stop eating. The feeling of fullness also comes from hormones released by the small intestine during digestion.

20 minutes the approximate amount of time it takes for the body to feel full once you start to eat

When the bladder and rectum are full of urine and faeces, sensors in their walls send a message to the brain. The brain creates the sensation that we need to go to the toilet.

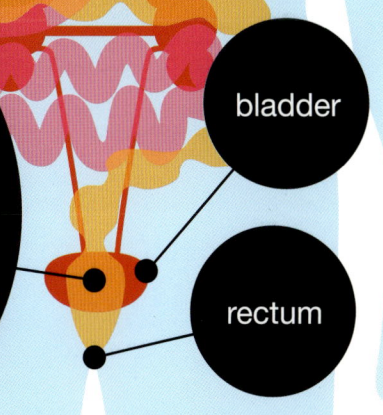

brain

stomach

bladder

rectum

Problems with senses

People can have issues with any of the senses, but sight and hearing issues are the most common. In some cases they can be treated with glasses, surgery or devices, such as hearing aids and implants.

Two common problems with sight are short- and long-sightedness. A short-sighted person will see close objects clearly, but distant objects will be blurry, while a long-sighted person has the opposite problem. These issues are caused by a problem with the shape of the eye, which means that light can't focus properly on the retina. They can be treated with glasses or by changing the shape of the cornea with lasers.

People who are short-sighted have eyeballs that are too long. This means that light rays focus in front of the retina, making objects appear blurry.

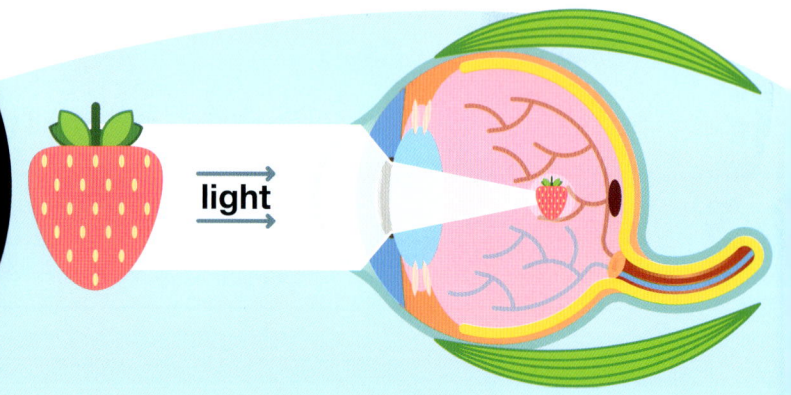

People who are long-sighted have eyeballs that are too short. This means that light rays focus behind the retina, making objects appear blurry.

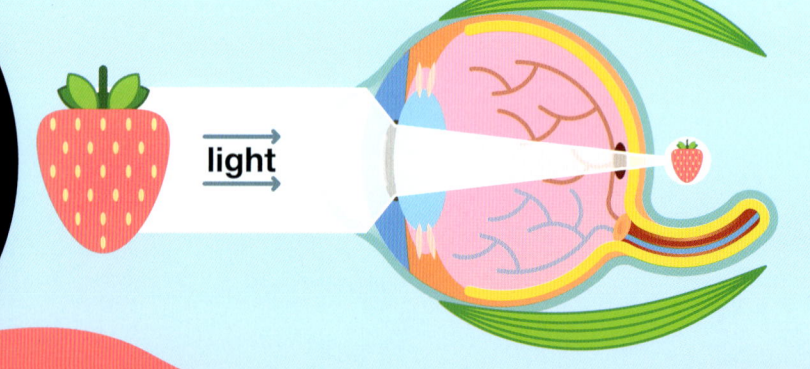

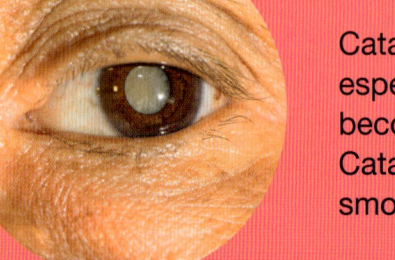

Cataracts are another common sight problem, especially among elderly people. The lens becomes cloudy, which can reduce vision. Cataracts are caused by many factors including smoking, injury to the eye and old age.

Some people are born deaf or with hearing loss, while others lose their hearing as the result of an injury or illness. Our hearing also gets worse as we get older, as the sensory cells in our ears are damaged over time. Standard hearing aids can help some people with mild hearing loss to hear more.

For people with severe hearing loss, a device such as a cochlear implant may be necessary. A cochlear implant converts sound waves into electrical signals that go straight to the auditory nerve and on to the brain, bypassing the body's hearing system. Some people in the Deaf community choose not to use any devices that help with hearing. They communicate via sign language or lip reading.

An external transmitter receives information about sounds from the speech processor and turns it into electrical signals.

Electrodes stimulate the auditory nerve, sending electrical signals along the nerve to the brain, where they are understood as sounds.

The external microphone picks up sound waves.

Electrical signals are sent from the receiver to a group of electrodes in the cochlea.

The internal receiver picks up signals from the transmitter.

A speech processor filters sounds to focus on speech.

466 million
the number of people worldwide with some degree of hearing loss, which is 5 per cent of the global population

Glossary

amplitude – the distance from the rest position to the top of a sound wave

binocular vision – the combined, overlapping sight from two eyes that allows us to see objects in depth

carbon dioxide – a waste gas produced by cells

cell – the smallest living part of a living thing

effector – a part of the body that produces a response, such as a muscle or a gland

gland – an organ that produces and releases substances in the body

hormones – chemicals that control important processes in the body

internal – inside the body

membrane – a thin layer of tissue

molecule – the smallest unit of a substance

motor neurone – a nerve cell that carries signals from the central nervous system to muscles or glands

odour – a smell

oxygen – a gas found in the air that cells need to produce energy

papillae – bumps on the tongue that contain taste buds

pitch – how high or low a sound is

proprioception – the sense of the position and strength of the body

receptor – a specialised cell that senses changes in the environment

reflex – a quick, involuntary response to stimuli

sensory neurone – a nerve cell that carries signals from receptors to the central nervous system

spinal cord – a long, thin tube inside the bones in the spine that contains billions of neurones

Further information

Books

Super Senses (Science is Everywhere) by Rob Colson (Wayland, 2018)

Senses (Human Body, Animal Bodies) by Izzi Howell (Wayland, 2017)

Taking Control: The Brain and Senses by Thomas Canavan (Franklin Watts, 2015)

Websites

www.sciencekids.co.nz/sciencefacts/humanbody/senses.html
Find out fun facts about the senses.

www.bbc.co.uk/programmes/p069jpyz
Watch a video about the sense of touch in animals and plants.

kidshealth.org/en/kids/experiment-main.html
Do some experiments to learn more about the senses.

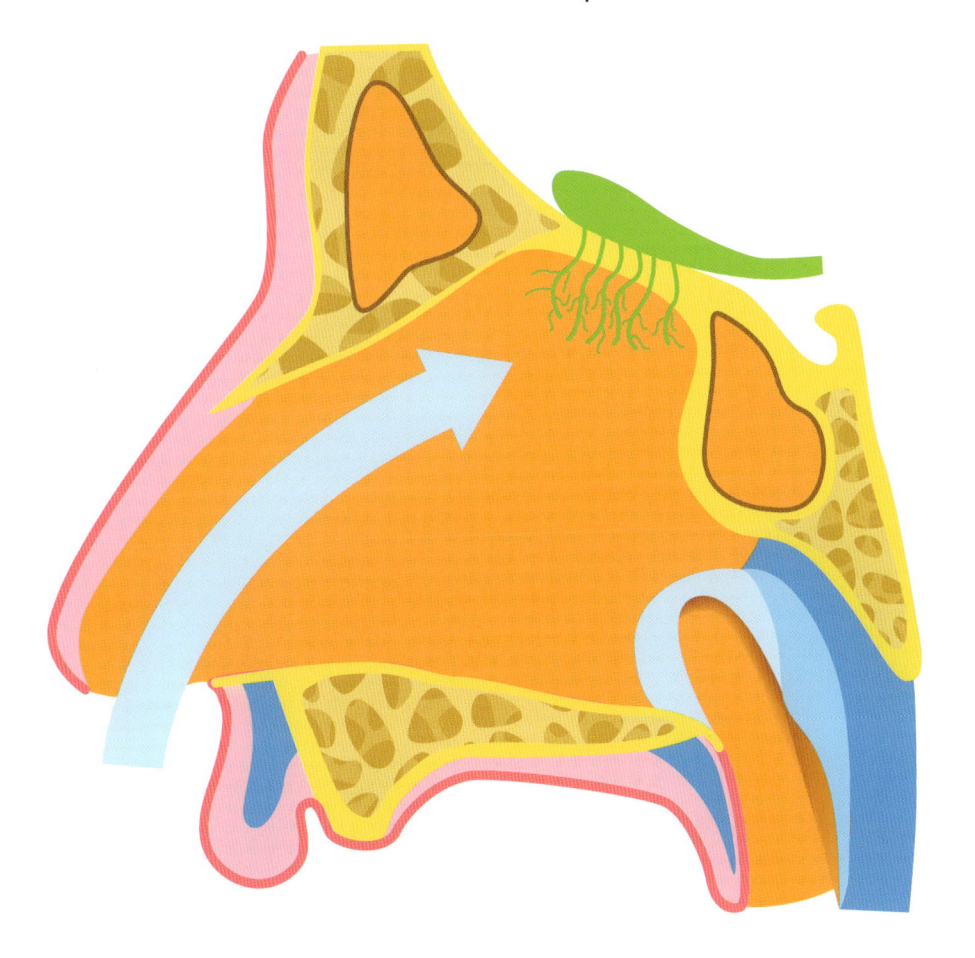

Index

balance 22, 23

binocular vision 9

brain 4, 5, 6, 7, 9, 10, 11, 14, 17, 21, 22, 23, 24–25, 26, 27, 29

brainstem 24

cataracts 28

cochlea 10, 11, 13, 23, 29

cochlear implants 29

ears 4, 10, 11, 13, 23, 24, 29

eyes 4, 6, 7, 8, 9, 22, 24, 28

field of vision 8

hearing 4, 10–11, 12–13, 28, 29

hearing loss 13, 28, 29

internal senses 26–27

mouth 4, 14, 24

muscles 8, 20, 21, 22, 24, 25

nerves 4, 6, 7, 10, 11, 14, 17, 21, 23, 24, 25, 29

nose 4, 16, 17, 22, 24

pain 18, 19, 20–21

pitch 12, 13

proprioception 22

reflexes 21

rods and cones 7

semicircular canals 10, 11, 23

sight 4, 5, 6–7, 8–9, 24, 28

sight issues 5, 28

skin 4, 5, 18, 19, 20, 21, 24

smell 4, 5, 15, 16–17, 24, 25

sound waves 10, 11, 12, 29

taste 4, 14–15, 17

taste buds 14, 15

tongue 14, 15

touch 4, 18–19, 20, 21

volume 4, 12, 13

TITLES IN THE SERIES

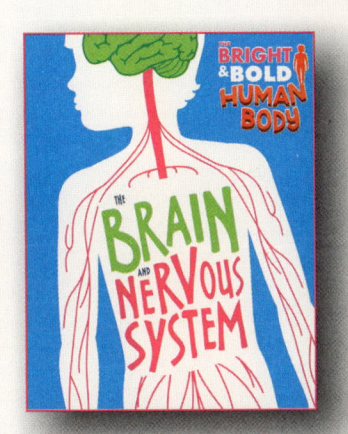

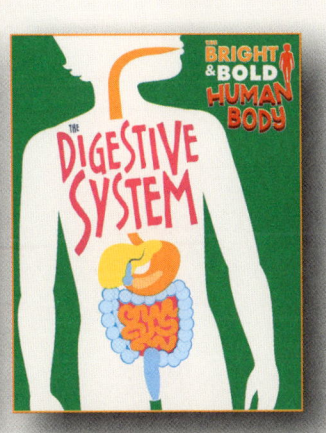

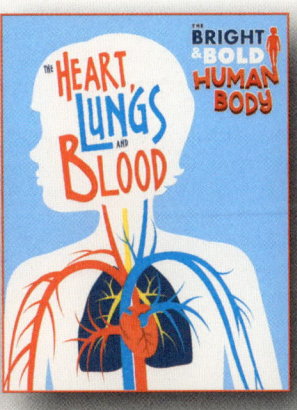

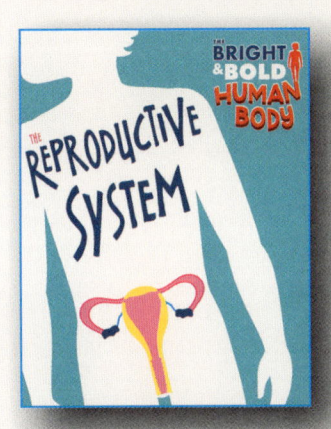

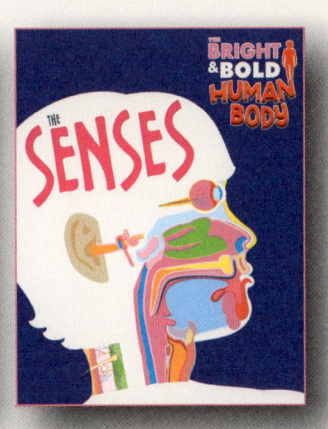

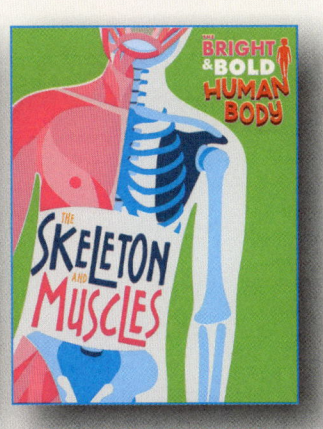

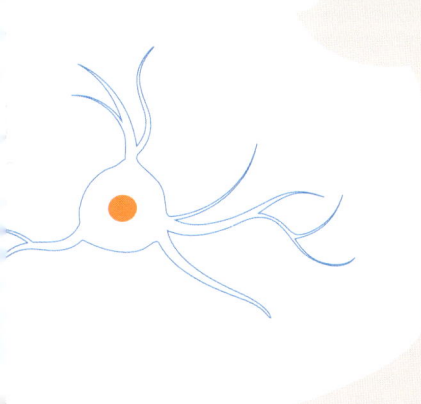

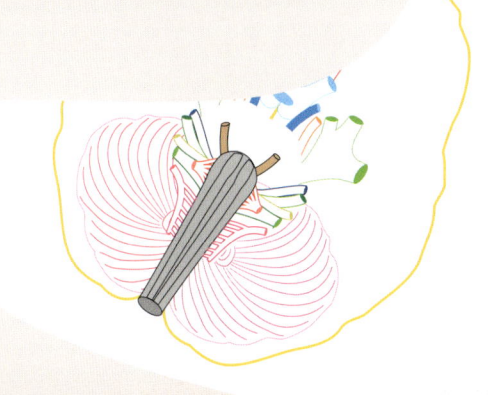

The Brain and Nervous System
9781526310408

The Digestive System
9781526310132

The Heart, Lungs and Blood
9781526310415

The Reproductive System
9781526310453

The Senses
9781526310446

The Skeleton and Muscles
9781526310378